Christmas
ABC

Christmas
ABC

Adapted from a poem by Carolyn Wells (1862–1942)

THE BRITISH MUSEUM PRESS

in association with

THE METROPOLITAN MUSEUM OF ART

A is
for Angel
who graces
the tree.

B is for
Bells that
chime out
in glee.

C is
for Candle
to light
Christmas Eve.

D is
for Dreams
that we
truly believe.

C. KREN

E is for
Evergreens
cut for
the room.

F is for
Flowers of
exquisite
perfume.

G is for
Gifts that
bring us
delight.

H is for Holly with red berries bright.

I is
for Ice,
so shining
and clear.

J is
for Joy
at this time
of year.

K is for
Kings who
came a
long way.

L is for
Lights that
brighten
the day.

M is
for Mother,
who's trimming
the bough.

N is for
Night, see
the stars
sparkling now.

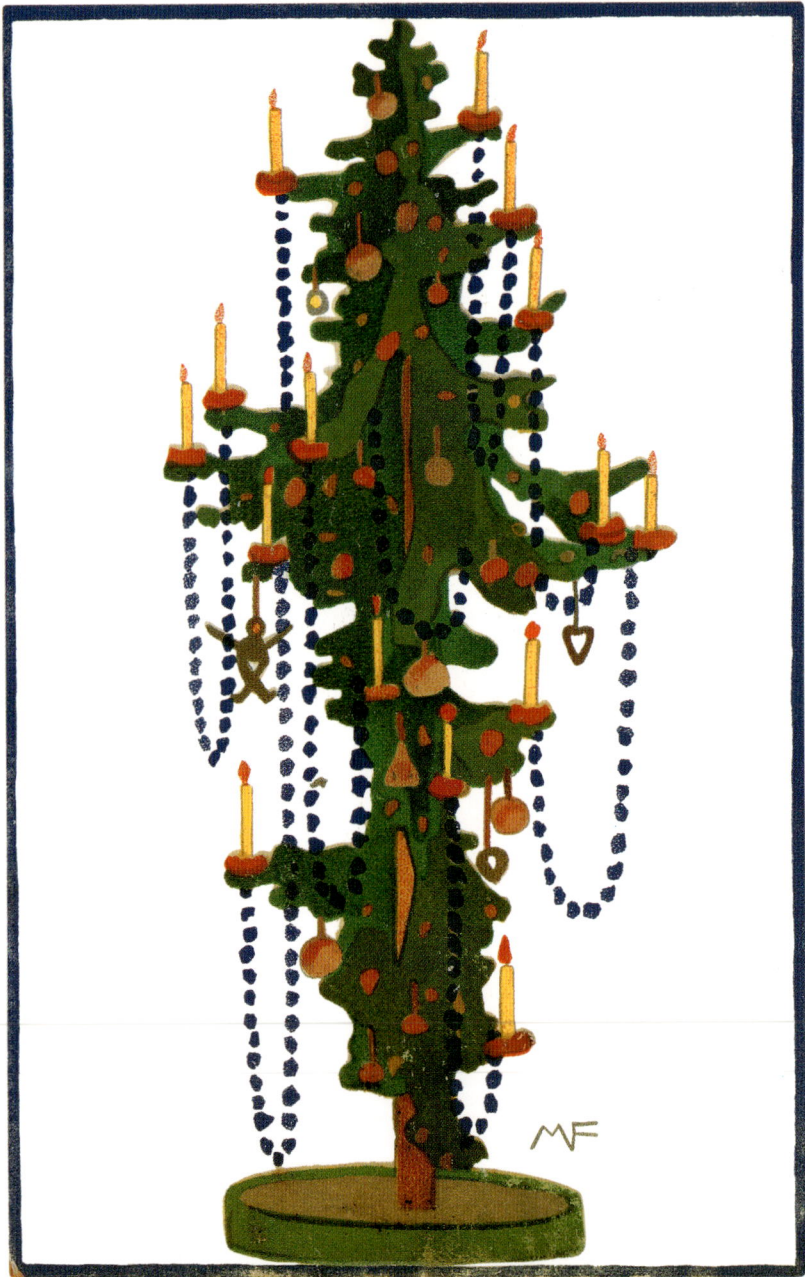

O is for
Ornaments,
dazzling
with light.

P is
for Parties
with friends
Christmas
night.

Q is
Quadrille, a
dance we
will do.

R is for
Ribbons,
bright red,
green, and
blue.

S is for
Snow that
falls silently
down.

T is for
Toys that
old Santa
brings 'round.

U is for
Uproar
that goes
on all day.

V is for
Voices that
sing out
and pray.

W is for Wreaths to be hung in the hall.

X is for
Xmas, with
pleasures
for all.

Y is for
Yuletide,
and may
yours be
bright.

Z is for
Zest shown
from morning
till night.

The illustrations reproduced in this book are from color lithographic postcards
designed by artists at the Wiener Werkstätte, in Vienna, Austria, between late 1907 and 1914.
All of the works of art are from the Department of Drawings and Prints of
The Metropolitan Museum of Art, New York.

Published in Great Britain in 2002 by The British Museum Press
A division of The British Museum Company Ltd
46 Bloomsbury Street, London WCIB 3QQ
Copyright © 2002 by The Metropolitan Museum of Art

First Edition
Printed in Hong Kong
11 10 09 08 07 06 05 04 03 02   5 4 3 2 1

ISBN 0 7141 2778 7

Produced by the Department of Special Publications, The Metropolitan Museum of Art:
Robie Rogge, Publishing Manager; Judith Cressy, Project Editor; Anna Raff, Designer.
All photography by The Metropolitan Museum of Art Photograph Studio.

Visit The British Museum Company Web site: www.britishmuseum.co.uk

A catalogue record for this book is available from The British Library